STANDOUT SAINTS

For my parents, Shawn and Stephanie, true pioneers,
and for Standout Saints everywhere who inspire us
—*SW*

To Shawn-Michael, and the others standing in light and truth,
who are willing to be seen and to inspire.
—*EST*

© 2020 Sierra Wilson
Illustrations © Emily Krogue Tueller

Library of Congress Cataloging-in-Publication Data
(CIP data on file)
ISBN 978-1-62972-806-3

Printed in China   6/2020
RR Donnelley, Dongguan, China

10 9 8 7 6 5 4 3 2 1

STANDOUT SAINTS

CHURCH HISTORY HEROES
— FROM —
AROUND THE WORLD

WRITTEN BY SIERRA WILSON ★ ILLUSTRATED BY EMILY SHAY TUELLER

DESERET BOOK

CONTENTS

CHURCH AND WORLD HISTORY TIMELINE

1820—Joseph Smith's First Vision

1830—Book of Mormon is published, and Church is officially organized

1830–1831—Saints are commanded to gather in Ohio

1833—Saints flee Jackson County, Missouri, due to persecution

1836—Kirtland Temple is dedicated

1837—First missionaries are sent to Great Britain

1842—First Relief Society is organized in Nauvoo

1844—Joseph and Hyrum Smith are martyred at Carthage Jail

1846—Saints begin to move to the West

1847—Brigham Young arrives in Salt Lake Valley

1867—Relief Society is reorganized in Utah

1875—Brigham Young Academy (now BYU) is established

1876—First missionaries arrive in Mexico

1878—First Primary meeting is held

1882—Deseret Hospital opens

1893—Salt Lake Temple is dedicated

1895—First stake outside the United States is established in Cardston, Alberta, Canada

1896—Utah achieves statehood

1901—Japan is dedicated and opened for missionary work

1912—First seminary program is established at Granite High School

1914–1918—World War I

1919—Laie Hawaii Temple is dedicated, first temple outside continental United States

1925—South America is dedicated for preaching of the gospel

1939–1945—World War II

1947—Church membership reaches one million

1955—Swiss Temple is dedicated, first temple in Europe

1958—New Zealand Temple is dedicated, first temple in South Pacific

1970—First stake in Africa is established in Transvaal, South Africa; first stake in Asia is established in Tokyo, Japan

1978—Revelation is received making priesthood available to all worthy male members; São Paulo Brazil Temple is dedicated, first temple in Latin America

1985—Johannesburg South Africa Temple is dedicated, first temple in Africa

1989—Fall of the Berlin Wall

1995—"The Family: A Proclamation to the World" is released

1997—Church membership reaches ten million

2000—The hundred millionth copy of the Book of Mormon is printed; Boston Massachusetts Temple is dedicated, becoming the one hundredth operating temple

2010—Kyiv Ukraine Temple opens, first temple built in a former Soviet Union nation

2020—The Church continues to grow throughout the world and celebrates the two-hundredth anniversary of Joseph Smith's First Vision; "The Restoration of the Fulness of the Gospel of Jesus Christ: A Bicentennial Proclamation to the World" is released

INTRODUCTION

What makes a Standout Saint? Awards? Fame? Worldwide recognition? Although many of the Saints in this book did achieve recognition and fame, others are less well known. Yet something makes them all stand out. That "something" is courageous faith. Each Saint in this book faced trials, from mob persecution to imprisonment, from loneliness and hunger to illness and death. But each of them chose to live by faith. They all chose to trust God, press forward, count their blessings, and do good during their time on earth.

I hope that as you read this book, the Saints you discover will inspire you. President M. Russell Ballard, a modern descendant of Hyrum Smith, said: "The Spirit has confirmed to me the important responsibility we have to see that the legacy of faith of our pioneer forefathers is never lost. We can derive great strength, particularly our youth, from understanding our Church history." As I've had the privilege of studying deeply the lives of past Saints, I've gained my own testimony that President Ballard's statement is true. The Saints who sacrificed, struggled, and rejoiced before us have left us with a rich legacy of faith and with powerful spiritual examples that can guide and inspire us today. They are a part of us, and we are a part of them, regardless of physical ancestry. As we follow their examples, we can be strong and courageous too.

As you read this book, I hope you will find new friends and heroes. Even more, I hope you will be inspired to become a pioneer yourself. Blaze new trails and do good, seeking God's guidance. Endure your trials with faith, just like these pioneers did. As you will see in this book, there are many different ways to serve God, make a difference, and live by courageous faith. These are the last days, and God has a special work for each of us to do. Study and pray to learn what God has in mind for you.

I also hope you'll be inspired to study more of Church history and your own family history. When you do, you'll feel closer to your ancestors, and you may even feel them reaching out to you.

There are so many Church history heroes out there; selecting only forty for this work was one of my greatest challenges. There are also many more wonderful stories not in this book about each of these heroes. I hope you'll start digging and find out more! If you find any great stories, I'd love to hear them. You can share them on my social media or contact me through my website: sierrawilsonauthor.com. (You'll also find on that website a complete list of the sources for the stories I've shared.)

Now it's your turn to go forth and be a Standout Saint!

LUCY MACK SMITH

1775–1856

"For I do testify that God has revealed himself to man again in these last days, and set his hand to gather his people."

Lucy grew up in a home full of love and faith, where she especially enjoyed stories of her father's adventures as a soldier. When she was a teenager, her older sisters developed a deadly disease, tuberculosis. Lucy carefully took care of them for years until they died. A few years later, she developed tuberculosis too. All the doctors believed Lucy would die, but she didn't give up hope. Lucy prayed with all her heart that God would heal her, promising to serve Him always. Then Lucy heard a voice say, "Seek and ye shall find; knock, and it shall be opened unto you. Let your heart be comforted." She was healed within the hour.

Years later, after embracing the gospel her son Joseph helped restore, Lucy led a group of eighty Saints from New York to Ohio during the frigid weather of early spring. They traveled along the bitter-cold Erie Canal with little food. When they reached Buffalo, New York, the harbor was covered in ice. They were stuck. Her group started arguing and complaining, but Lucy bore her bold testimony: "If you will all of you raise your desires to heaven, that the ice may be broken up, and we be set at liberty, as sure as the Lord lives, it will be done." Moments later, the ice parted, and she and her group were able to continue safely on their journey.

For the rest of her life, Lucy did all she could to help build up the kingdom of God. She suffered many sorrows, including the deaths of her husband and several children, but she held firmly to her faith. Lucy spent her life caring for others and was fondly known as "Mother Smith," a faithful woman who kept her promises to God.

EDWARD PARTRIDGE

1793-1840

"I will rejoice and praise my Father in heaven, that he has permitted me to live in this day and age, when I can see the work of the Lord and know it for myself."

Edward was a successful and well-respected hatmaker in Ohio, but he longed for something more. When four Latter-day Saint missionaries showed up at his store, at first he sent them away. But then he felt something. He sent one of his employees after the men to purchase a copy of the Book of Mormon. Edward started investigating the Church, even traveling to New York to learn more. While there, he met Joseph Smith and asked to be baptized. He had found what he was seeking and held onto it like a treasure.

Just two months after his baptism, Edward was called as the first bishop of the Church. This was a huge challenge. Edward had the difficult job of caring for the new Saints arriving in Ohio, many of whom were poor and fleeing their previous homes. Edward was responsible for managing the bishop's storehouse, distributing food and goods to the needy, purchasing and distributing land, and more.

Along with his duties as bishop, Edward also faced persecution and violence. One day, Edward and another Saint, Charles Allen, were seized by a mob. The mob demanded that they either renounce the Book of Mormon or leave the county, giving up their homes and land. Edward and Charles refused, and so the mob covered their bodies with hot tar and feathers. Throughout the painful torture, Edward and Charles remained so calm that their persecutors felt guilty and walked away. Later, Edward said, "I feel willing to spend and be spent, in the cause of my blessed Master."

Edward and his family eventually settled in Nauvoo with the Saints. There Edward continued serving as bishop until he died of illness. Later, in a revelation recorded in Doctrine and Covenants 124:19, the Lord revealed that Edward was with Him in heaven.

PATTY BARTLETT SESSIONS

1795–1892

*"I feel to thank the Lord that I have passed through what I have.
I have gained an experience I could not have gained no other way."*

As a young woman, Patty trained to be a midwife, helping to deliver women's babies. Her first successful delivery actually happened before she had even finished her training! The local midwife couldn't walk fast enough, so she told Patty to rush ahead, and she delivered the new baby safely. The doctor praised Patty as a natural and said she would have a prosperous career. He was right—she went on to deliver thousands of babies.

After Patty joined the Church, she went west with the other Saints. Along the way, she used her medical skills to help her fellow travelers. She delivered many babies on the trek through the wilderness and cared for Saints with ailments from blistered feet to fevers. Patty wrote in her journal, "My health is poor, my mind weighed down, but my heart is in God." Even though she was often tired herself, sometimes she rode back several miles along the trail to help deliver a baby or ease a sickness.

When she finally reached the Salt Lake Valley, Patty delivered the first baby boy in Zion, just as she'd been told she would in a special prophecy. Patty said, "I have come more than one thousand miles to do it since [the promise] was spoken."

After Patty arrived in Utah, she continued working as a midwife and set up a school, called the Patty Sessions Academy, that allowed poor children to attend for free. She endured the deaths of several of her children yet continued to love and serve others. She worked hard to follow God and donated money to help other Saints move west. Patty lived strong in love and faith to the end of her days at age ninety-seven.

HYRUM SMITH

1800–1844

"I thank God that I felt a determination to die, rather than deny the things which my eyes had seen, which my hands had handled, and which I had born testimony to."

Hyrum loved his family dearly and always tried to take care of them. Throughout his life, he had a special relationship with his younger brother Joseph. Once, when the boys were young, Joseph was very sick and had to have leg surgery to remove an infection. Hyrum sat beside him and held his leg for days to ease the pain. Later, Hyrum believed in Joseph's call from the Lord and developed his own powerful testimony of the restored gospel.

Hyrum helped in Joseph's work in any way he could. He oversaw much of the printing of the Book of Mormon, carrying the manuscript piece by piece, buttoned safely inside his own coat, to the printing office. In the middle of the printing process, Hyrum began to feel uneasy. One Sunday, when the office should have been closed, he felt he needed to go there. When he arrived, he discovered a man illegally printing portions of the Book of Mormon for his newspaper. Hyrum stood up to the man and said, "That manuscript is sacred, and I forbid your printing any more of it." Because Hyrum listened to the Spirit, he was able to protect and defend the Book of Mormon.

Hyrum continued to serve God and help Joseph all his life. Joseph relied on him deeply and said of him, "Brother Hyrum, what a faithful heart you have got." He served as one of the Eight Witnesses of the Book of Mormon, a member of the First Presidency, and a patriarch. He eventually chose to go with Joseph to Carthage Jail, where they were both killed for their faith. In a revelation recorded in Doctrine and Covenants 124:15, the Lord said, "Blessed is my servant Hyrum Smith; for I, the Lord, love him because of the integrity of his heart, and because he loveth that which is right before me."

MARY FIELDING SMITH

1801-1852

"Blessed be the God and Rock of my salvation,
here I am, and am perfectly satisfied and happy, having
not the smallest desire to go one step backward."

As a girl raised on a farm in England, Mary learned to work hard and have faith in God. Those early lessons would serve her well in her future. After accepting the gospel in Canada, Mary moved to Kirtland, Ohio. She soon married Hyrum Smith, whose wife had died, leaving him with five children. Along with Hyrum, Mary suffered many persecutions and had to flee from home to home. She endured extreme illness and the death of her dear husband, but Mary remained strong and faithful.

After Hyrum's death, Mary's challenges were far from over, but the Lord saw her through. She and her family joined the Saints on the long journey west. At the beginning, she asked her group's captain for help. He told her to turn back, saying she would be a burden on the journey. Mary was determined to go west with the Saints and said, "I will beat you to the valley and ask for no help either." Mary pressed on, prayed with faith, and experienced miracles. At one point, her ox, Old Buck, became very sick. The group's captain told Mary the ox was dying and to leave it behind. Instead of losing hope, Mary got a bottle of consecrated oil and found two brothers to bless her ox. Old Buck jumped right up, healthy and well. In spite of other mishaps, Mary did beat the captain to the Salt Lake Valley.

In Utah, Mary chose her own homestead and got to work. Though she had little, she paid her tithing with her best potatoes, saying she trusted in the Lord and His blessings. She raised her children to have strong faith. Her son Joseph F., who became the sixth President of the Church, summed up her character well: "She was good! She was pure! She was indeed a Saint! A royal daughter of God."

BRIGHAM YOUNG

1801–1877

*"I wanted to thunder and roar out the Gospel to the nations.
It burned in my bones like fire pent up, so I [commenced]
to preach the gospel of life to the people."*

Brigham was a builder in every sense of the word. As a young man, he became an expert carpenter, respected for his reliability and skill. Later, he would become a builder of temples, a builder of towns, and, most important, a builder of the kingdom of God.

In his early years, Brigham deeply desired more spiritual knowledge but could not find it. When he heard of the restored gospel, he carefully pondered and studied it for two years. At one point he prayed, "If this religion is true, send the missionaries to my home, that they might pray for my sick wife and also explain the gospel to her." The missionaries came the next day. Soon after, Brigham and all his family joined the Church.

After escaping persecution and fleeing to Nauvoo, Brigham was called to serve a mission to England. At that time, he was so ill he could hardly walk. His sister begged him not to go, but he was determined to accept the call, saying, "My firm resolve was that I would do what I was required to do in the Gospel of life and salvation, or I would die trying to do it." In England, he went on to witness miracles as thousands joined the Church and the kingdom of God grew and grew.

Brigham earned the nickname "the Lion of the Lord" and lived up to it through his strong testimony and courageous commitment to truth in the face of hardship and persecution. He oversaw the migration of more than sixty thousand pioneers and the founding of hundreds of settlements throughout the West. Brigham served as prophet and Church President for thirty years, the longest of any latter-day prophet, giving his life to serving the Lord and the people he loved.

ELIZA R. SNOW

1804–1887

"An ordeal furnace near at hand,
Will test your faith and texture too;
But God will give you grace to stand,
And He will help you safely through."

Eliza was raised in a strong family and received a good education. She especially loved to write poetry. When she learned about the restored gospel, she studied it carefully for six years before deciding to be baptized. After her baptism, she saw a special vision of a candle burning above her feet. She asked to know what the vision meant and received the answer: "The lamp of intelligence shall be lighted over your path."

Eliza and other faithful Saints were driven from one home to the next by angry mobs. One freezing December day, as they fled more persecution in Missouri, Eliza walked ahead of the wagons, trying to warm her frozen feet. A member of the Missouri militia approached her and said, "Well, I think this will cure you of your faith." Eliza looked him boldly in the eye and replied, "No, sir, it will take more than this to cure me of my faith." The man was shocked and said she was a much better soldier than he was.

Later, when Eliza was preparing to flee yet another home to journey west, she paused to write one of her most beloved poems. The poem, now known as the hymn "O My Father," teaches powerful lessons about premortal, mortal, and eternal life and our Heavenly Parents.

Throughout her life, Eliza remained true to the gospel and served the Lord in many ways. She wrote hundreds of poems to preach the gospel, share the story of the Saints, and uplift others, becoming known as "Zion's poetess." She served as the second Relief Society General President and helped found the Primary and Young Women programs. She defended the Church, served in the temple, and developed the first Primary curriculum. Eliza let the Spirit of the Lord light her path and strengthen her faith.

HEBER C. KIMBALL

1801-1868

"I put my trust in God,
believing that He would assist me."

Heber, a blacksmith and potter by trade, was a simple man, but God had a great destiny planned for him. As a young man, he had yearned to find God's truth. After finding the restored gospel, he held fast to it and remained loyal and valiant through all the challenges and trials of the early Church years.

In Kirtland, Heber was called to the first Quorum of the Twelve Apostles in the latter days. Then, in 1837, he received a special call to take the gospel to England. Heber felt overwhelmed by the mission call but chose to rely on God. He prayed daily in the temple for strength. He said, "The moment I understood the will of my Heavenly Father, I felt a determination to go at all hazards, believing that He would support me by His almighty power, and endow me with every qualification needed." He blessed his family, trusting that God would watch over them, and left for England, going without money or many belongings. His mission was filled with miracles. Within a few days of arriving, Heber and his companions found and baptized new converts. In just a few months, more than a thousand people joined the fold of God. Heber said that some days his clothes were never dry because he was performing so many baptisms. Later, Heber would return with other companions to England, and many thousands more would join the Church, strengthening the kingdom of God on the earth.

In total, Heber served eight missions for the Lord. He also journeyed in the first trek to the Salt Lake Valley and served as first counselor to President Brigham Young for nearly twenty years. Heber's powerful faith held firm, and he served the Lord to his last breath.

EMMA HALE SMITH

1804-1879

*"I feel a divine trust in God,
that all things shall work for good."*

As a young girl, Emma worried that her father didn't have strong faith in Jesus Christ, so she went into the woods to pray for him. When her father overheard her, his heart was touched, and his faith was strengthened. Throughout her life, Emma would continue to touch hearts and strengthen others' faith as she played a key role in building up God's kingdom on earth.

One example of her faith and courage came while her husband, Joseph, was imprisoned in Liberty Jail. Emma and the other Saints had to flee Missouri during the harsh winter. As they left, Emma crossed the frozen Mississippi River with her four young children, two in her arms and two clinging to her sides. Around her waist she had tied hidden bags holding Joseph's translation of the Bible. Her courage helped protect her family and preserve sacred writings from the Lord.

Another example of Emma's strength and service was how she opened her home to others. Even though she had her own children to care for, Emma had a big heart and often had many extra people staying in her home, including the hungry, homeless, and ill. Sometimes she and Joseph even gave up their own beds and slept in a tent in the yard to give more room to the needy.

Although Emma suffered through the deaths of many of her young children and her dear husband, she also experienced great miracles and felt God's love. She filled important roles such as serving as a scribe for the Book of Mormon translation, compiling the Church's first hymn book, and leading as the president of the first Relief Society. Throughout many personal trials, Emma lifted Joseph and the other Saints. She truly was "an elect lady" (Doctrine and Covenants 25:3).

JOSEPH SMITH JR.

1805–1844

"God Almighty is my shield; and what can man do if God is my friend? I shall not be sacrificed until my time comes; then I shall be offered freely."

As a young boy, Joseph wanted to know which was God's true Church. He asked questions, searched the scriptures, pondered, and prayed. Finally, after reading in James 1:5, "If any of you lack wisdom, let him ask of God," Joseph knew what he needed to do. He went to a quiet place in the woods and prayed, asking God which church he should join. Heavenly Father and Jesus Christ appeared to Joseph. They taught him that God's true Church was lost on the earth but that it would soon be restored. Joseph was called as the prophet to begin God's work in the latter days.

Throughout his life, Joseph was known for his great kindness and strong faith. On many occasions, enemies became his friends when they got to know him. Once, while he was at his parents' home, a group of armed men came and threatened to kill him. Surprisingly, Joseph smiled at them and shook their hands. Then he explained to them about the restored gospel and the persecution the Saints had endured. After talking for a time, Joseph said he needed to go home because his wife, Emma, would be waiting for him. Two of the men quickly rose and offered to escort him, saying it wasn't safe for him to be out alone. Joseph's mother overheard the other men talking about how they felt the Spirit in Joseph's presence and would never seek to harm him or any Saints again. Joseph's trust in God and loving heart made an impact wherever he went.

Through God's guidance, Joseph accomplished amazing things. He received hundreds of revelations, translated the Book of Mormon, built cities, restored temple covenants and saw Church membership grow from a small handful to 26,000. He suffered cruel and unjust treatment many times but always pressed on in the sacred work God had given him.

DESIDERIA QUINTANAR DE YÁÑEZ

1814–1893

*"I will pour out my spirit upon all flesh; . . . your old men
[and women] shall dream dreams." (Joel 2:28)*

Desideria, a Mexican descendant of one of the last Aztec emperors, lived most of her life without the gospel, but when the chance came to receive it, she accepted it with open arms.

When she was sixty-six years old, Desideria had a special dream. In her dream, she saw men publishing a pamphlet by Parley P. Pratt in Mexico City. She was told that the pamphlet would strengthen her spirit. The problem was that Mexico City was seventy-five miles away—an almost impossible distance for an old widow in poor health. But Desideria knew the dream was important. She told her son José about it, and he undertook the journey to Mexico City, where he found the men from his mother's dream—missionaries from the Church. The missionaries sent José home with several pamphlets and gospel tracts. Desideria studied all she had received and was touched by the Spirit. Soon, missionaries came out to Desideria's town of Nopala. She became the first woman baptized in Mexico.

Desideria and her family lived far from the Church colonies of northern Mexico, and she was never able to attend a ward or go to the temple. Nevertheless, she remained faithful, and soon more of her family chose to be baptized. A few years later, Desideria had a terrifying experience: thieves broke into her home, robbing and beating her. Desideria held to her faith and soon was visited by Elder Erastus Snow of the Twelve Apostles, who gave her a priesthood blessing. Not long after, she learned of the new Spanish translation of the Book of Mormon. She was so excited to read it that she was given an early unbound copy, becoming the first person to receive a Spanish Book of Mormon in Mexico. The words of the scriptures and her personal experiences with God's love and care strengthened her, and she remained faithful all her life, a stalwart pioneer.

ORSON HYDE

1805–1878

"Give [me] . . . a heart to choose the good . . . grace to endure all things for Thy name's sake."

As a young orphan boy, Orson walked six hundred miles to Kirtland, Ohio, seeking work. Before his life was through, he would travel tens of thousands of miles serving the Lord as a missionary. Not long after his baptism in Ohio, Orson was called on his first mission. Later, he was part of the first mission to England, in which thousands joined the Church, but his missionary service was not over yet.

Orson's most unusual mission was to Jerusalem. This was in fulfillment of a prophecy from Joseph Smith in which Orson was told he would go to Jerusalem and, with God's power, "do a good work, which shall prepare the way, and greatly facilitate the gathering together of that people." The journey to Jerusalem took nineteen challenging months, during which Orson experienced miracles. For example, a mysterious stranger donated a large sum of money that helped fund his travel. Orson also saw visions of the signs of the times. When he finally reached Jerusalem, he burst into tears. It was exactly as he had seen it in a vision. He climbed the Mount of Olives and offered a powerful prayer, dedicating the land for the return of the Jews and the building of a future temple. By the time he returned home, he had been gone 967 days and traveled more than twenty thousand miles, entrusting his family to God's care and braving many dangers. At the time, his was the longest mission that had ever been undertaken.

Back with the Saints, Orson continued to serve in both the Church and his communities. He served as an Apostle for forty-three years, founded new settlements in the West, edited newspapers, served in government positions, and more. In total, he served thirteen missions for the Lord and held true to his faith.

JANE MANNING JAMES

1822–1908

"I want to say right here, that my faith in the gospel of Jesus Christ . . . is as strong today, nay, it is if possible stronger than it was the day I was first baptized."

Jane began working as a servant when she was a young girl in Connecticut. She joined a local church but felt something was missing. When she heard missionaries preaching the restored gospel, she knew she had found what she lacked. Jane chose to be baptized, becoming one of the first African-American Saints.

After Jane was baptized, the Saints were gathering in Nauvoo. She and her family wanted to join the Saints there, so they walked over eight hundred miles, suffering pain, cold, and danger to follow God. During the journey, their shoes wore out and their feet began to leave bloody footprints on the ground. Jane said, "We stopped and united in prayer to the Lord, we asked God the Eternal Father to heal our feet." Heavenly Father heard their prayers, and their feet were miraculously healed.

When Jane reached Nauvoo, she and her family received a warm greeting from the Prophet Joseph and his wife, Emma. Jane said she recognized the prophet right away because she had seen him before in a dream. She knew she was where she needed to be.

Jane developed a close relationship with Joseph and Emma and was invited to live and work in their home. Later, she married and traveled with her new husband and the Saints to Utah. Along the way, Jane gave birth to a son in Winter Quarters. Though she had little food, at one point she shared half her flour with another sister in need. Jane settled in Utah and lived into her nineties. During her long life she experienced beautiful blessings and painful heartache, but through it all, she trusted her Heavenly Father.

ELIJAH ABEL

1810-1884

"Beloved, think it not strange concerning the fiery trial which is to try you." (1 Peter 4:12)

Elijah was a powerful missionary. After joining the Church, he served three missions in the US and Canada and was the first missionary with black African ancestry. Elijah was a humble man without much education, but he taught with the power of the Holy Ghost and trusted God.

Once, while serving as a missionary in Canada, he had a dream about a woman he had baptized in New York. In the dream, he saw that a woman named Sister Franklin couldn't eat or sleep because of her doubts about the Book of Mormon and Joseph Smith. Elijah returned to New York immediately. He invited Sister Franklin to hear him preach again at a nearby schoolhouse. She went and felt the Spirit strongly.

After the meeting, Elijah promised Sister Franklin he would return again in two weeks. But then some people began spreading terrible rumors about Elijah. Some people wanted to get rid of him. Even though it was dangerous, Elijah returned and kept his promise to preach. The schoolhouse was packed with people, many probably expecting him to be arrested or attacked. Yet Elijah stood up bravely before his audience. When he began teaching, he said, "If anyone has anything to do with me, now is your time. But after I commence my services, don't you dare to lay your hands on me." The Spirit in the room was strong, and no one harmed Elijah. He went on to preach a powerful sermon.

Elijah also served the Lord with his carpentry skills, helping build the Kirtland, Nauvoo, and Salt Lake Temples, even though, as a black African member, he was never able to receive his temple endowments during his lifetime. Elijah chose to hold fast to his faith in Jesus Christ and His Church and followed God to the end.

EMMELINE B. WELLS

1828–1921

*"Teach the peaceable things of the kingdom [and] look
after the needy more diligently than ever."*

As a young girl in Massachusetts, Emmeline loved to write poems and tell stories. She received a good education and dreamed of a literary future. Little did she know all the Lord had in store for her and how her talents would affect the world.

After joining the Church, Emmeline followed the Saints from Nauvoo to Utah. Her first husband had abandoned her, and her first baby and second husband both died. Emmeline could have let sorrow rule her life, but instead she turned to serving others. She became a leader in the fight for women's right to vote. She wrote many articles defending the women of the Church. Her tireless work got the attention of the nation, and Emmeline represented Utah in the National Woman Suffrage Association for nearly thirty years. She helped build bridges of understanding between Latter-day Saints and the rest of the country. At last, women's suffrage was included in the Utah constitution, making Utah one of the first states to grant women the right to vote.

In 1876, Brigham Young placed Emmeline in charge of a grain-saving program for the Church. It was difficult work, but Emmeline knew it was important. Years later, when Emmeline was serving as Relief Society General President, the Church was able to sell more than 200,000 bushels of saved wheat to the US government to help provide food during World War I. When the war ended, US President Woodrow Wilson visited Emmeline to thank her for sharing the Church's stored grain during a desperate time for the nation.

Emmeline lived a long life full of service. She wrote, "I have desired with all my heart to do those things that would advance women . . . and tend to the rolling on of the work of God upon the earth."

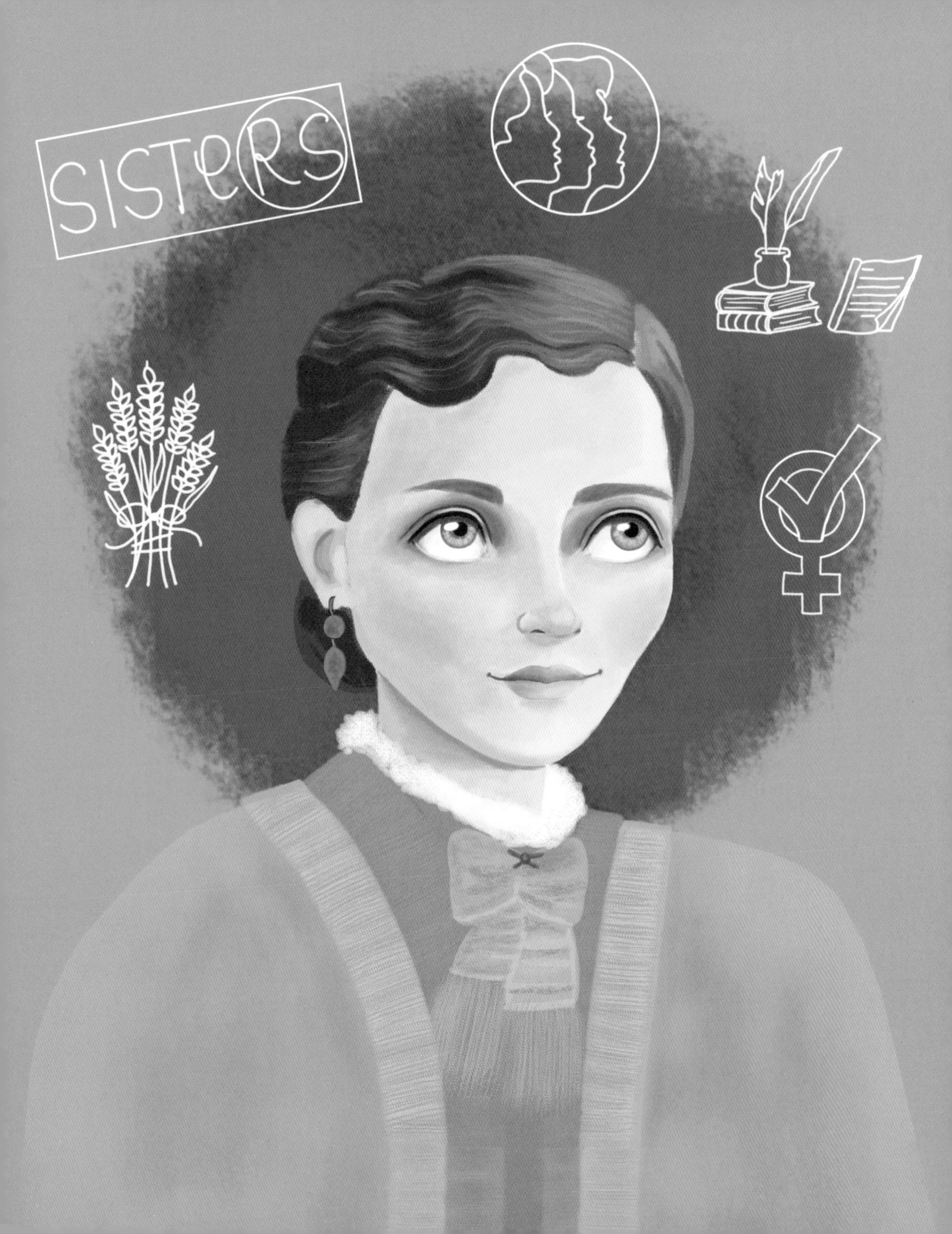
SISTERS

JONATANA NAPELA

1813-1879

"Seek wisdom and knowledge from the Lord and learn the right way ourselves and then we shall be prepared to teach others."

Jonatana, a Hawaiian chief of royal ancestry, had land and position, but chose to live a life of service. While serving as a district judge, Jonatana had a dream about a messenger in white coming with an important message. Meanwhile, the early Latter-day Saint missionaries to Hawaii were struggling to share the gospel. One elder, George Q. Cannon, prayed for direction and was guided to Jonatana, who soon became one of the first Hawaiian Saints. The two became close friends and went on to create the first Hawaiian translation of the Book of Mormon.

Jonatana faced persecution and lost his position as a judge because of being baptized, but he pressed forward with faith and turned his focus to missionary work. Jonatana knew the missionaries needed to learn Hawaiian to share the gospel, so he formed the first language training center for missionaries in his own home. He helped foreign missionaries learn Hawaiian for two months before they went out to preach. His ideas are still used in the Missionary Training Centers today.

Later in life, Jonatana was given permission from Hawaii's king to visit Utah. There he met Brigham Young and became the first Hawaiian to receive his temple endowments. A few years later, Jonatana's wife, Kitty, developed leprosy. At that time, Hawaiians with leprosy were sent to a leper colony on the island of Molokai to live until they died. Although he was healthy, Jonatana chose to go with Kitty and live in the leper colony. He eventually became the branch president of the Latter-day Saints there and worked hard to improve the lives of those suffering from leprosy. In time, Jonatana developed leprosy too, yet he kept his faith strong and served others to the end.

MARY BOMMELI

1831–1913

"Never did my home life run so smoothly . . . as those days when I stepped into the temple . . . each morning and out each evening."

Mary lived with her family on a small farm in Switzerland. She wove and sold cloth to help care for her family. When she was a young woman, she heard about the restored gospel. From the time she gained her testimony, Mary chose to live her faith boldly and bravely, no matter the consequences.

After Mary and her family were baptized, they wanted to move to America to gather with the Saints. The journey was expensive, and they couldn't afford to bring everyone. Mary volunteered to stay behind so her family could go. She had faith that she could earn money to make her own way. Mary moved to Germany and began working as a weaver. Preaching the gospel was illegal, but Mary couldn't help but share her testimony and beliefs with all around her. People gathered to hear her, and many hearts were touched. But soon the word got out that she was preaching, and Mary was thrown in jail. However, even this couldn't stop her from preaching. She wrote a letter to the judge of her trial and shared the gospel with him, too. Miraculously, his heart was softened, and Mary was set free.

Soon, Mary earned enough money to travel to America. The journey was long, but Mary found joy in it. In fact, she met her future husband, recently returned missionary Henry (Heinrich) Eyring, as they walked together across the plains to Utah. One of their great-grandchildren, Henry B. Eyring, would one day become First Counselor in the First Presidency of the Church. Mary's pioneer days did not end when she arrived in the Salt Lake Valley. She and her husband were called to help settle St. George and the Latter-day Saint colonies in Mexico. Throughout all her journeys and trials, Mary's faith sustained her. She served God and shared her faith to the end of her days.

WILLIAM CLAYTON

1814–1879

"I desire and strive, brethren, to keep my account right with the Lord every day that I may meet him with joy."

When William first heard of the restored gospel, he was a young man working as a clerk in England. William took a few weeks to gain a testimony, but when he did, he asked to be baptized right away. He was baptized that night at 11:00 p.m. in the River Ribble. From that point on, William put his whole heart into building up the kingdom.

After giving up his job and serving in the British mission presidency, William eventually joined the Saints in America. William was told in his patriarchal blessing that he would have a good memory and later received another blessing that "he should be a scribe for this church in the resurrection." William used his talents for record keeping when he was called by the Prophet Joseph Smith to serve as his personal clerk. William recorded important revelations and other sacred information. During this time, he got to know Joseph well and had a strong testimony of the Prophet.

Even after Joseph's death, William continued to use his record-keeping talents to build up God's kingdom. During the Saints' journey west, he served as a clerk for Brigham Young. He carefully tracked the terrain and miles of the journey, even helping invent an early version of the odometer to do so. He published his records of the trek as *The Latter-day Saints' Emigrants' Guide.* This guide helped thousands of pioneers journey across the plains.

Besides working as a record keeper, William also served in other ways, including through music. He played in concerts during the westward trek to lift the Saints' spirits. He also wrote the words to the beloved hymn "Come, Come, Ye Saints," which continues to inspire listeners to this day. Whether recording histories or writing songs, William dedicated his talents to the Lord and served faithfully all his days.

EMILY HILL WOODMANSEE

1836-1906

*"Our trust was in God,
and our strength was in prayer."*

Born in Warminster, England, Emily had a longing for truth even as a child. She studied the Bible and asked many questions but couldn't find the truth she was looking for. When her cousin invited her family to hear the Latter-day Saints preach, Emily decided to go, even though the rest of her family declined. She walked five miles to attend the meeting. What she heard changed her life. Emily had finally found the truth she was seeking.

Although Emily's parents never approved of her beliefs, she was finally baptized at age sixteen. Her older sister, Julia, was baptized, too. The girls worked for four years, saving money to join the Latter-day Saints in Zion. When Emily was only twenty years old, she and Julia set sail for America, leaving behind all they knew to follow their faith. The journey across the sea was long, but it was only the beginning. Soon, Emily and Julia joined the Willie handcart company. Emily and the other pioneers walked over a thousand miles, pulling their belongings in carts. Miraculously, Emily was able to walk every step of the way without ever riding in a wagon. Near the journey's end, the entire company was in danger of dying in the winter snow. Brave volunteers sent by Brigham Young went out to help bring the company to Utah. One of the rescuers cried when he saw how starved Emily looked. He offered her an onion, but she gave it to another pioneer who was near death. That pioneer later said the onion saved his life.

Throughout her life, Emily's faith burned bright, and she shared her testimony and stories in hundreds of poems and other writings. One of her poems became the words for the beloved hymn "As Sisters in Zion," still sung throughout the world today.

GIUSEPPE TARANTO (JOSEPH TORONTO)

1818-1883

"His life inspires me. He was a good man, full of faith, commitment and integrity." (Mary Christensen, one of Giuseppe's modern-day descendants)

Giuseppe was born in Sicily, Italy, and worked as a sailor and fisherman. As a young man, he saved his wages and earned enough money to go to America.

During the voyage to America, Giuseppe became nervous that his money would be stolen. He had a special dream in which he was told that if he took his money to "Mormon Brigham," he and his family would be blessed. When Giuseppe landed in New York, he tried to find information about "Mormon Brigham" but could discover nothing. Later, he moved to Boston and began his own business. While there, he met the missionaries and finally learned who Brigham was. Giuseppe also learned about the restored gospel. His heart was touched, and he decided to be baptized, becoming the first Italian convert to the Church.

At that time, the Saints were in Nauvoo, and the missionaries counseled Giuseppe to move there. However, his business was doing well, and he chose to stay in Boston. Later on, he nearly died in an accident and decided it was time to join the Saints in Nauvoo. He would arrive at the perfect moment. The Prophet Joseph Smith had just been killed, and the Saints were struggling to complete the Nauvoo Temple. Giuseppe heard Brigham Young announce that work on the temple would have to be stopped due to lack of funds. Two days later, Giuseppe donated more than two thousand dollars in gold, his life savings, to help complete the temple. He wanted to give all he had to building up the kingdom of God. Brigham Young was touched and pronounced a blessing on Giuseppe.

Because of Giuseppe and other Saints' sacrifices, the Nauvoo Temple was soon completed. Giuseppe continued to serve faithfully and give all he had to God. Eventually, he traveled to Italy as one of the first missionaries to his native land.

ELLIS REYNOLDS SHIPP

1847–1939

"By the aid of my Heavenly Father I hope to make my life one of usefulness upon the earth."

After crossing the plains to Utah with her family at age five, Ellis lost her mother at age fourteen. This was a great trial, the first of many challenging experiences Ellis had with death that would help her develop compassion and a deep desire to serve.

Ellis had a longing to learn. As a girl, she sewed a large pocket into her dress so she could carry the dictionary with her and study. After she married, she chose to get up at 4:00 a.m. each day and study different subjects for three hours before everyone else woke. While Ellis was still a young mother, she was encouraged to go to medical school in the East. Although Ellis would greatly miss her young children, she prayed and sought the Lord's will. She felt that He desired her to go, so she heeded the call. For the next three years, Ellis lived on bread and milk and studied long hours. She also worked as a seamstress and even a night guard to earn money for her schooling. She pressed through all her challenges and continued trusting in God. With His help, she graduated with high honors, becoming one of Utah's first female doctors.

Back home, Ellis set up her own medical clinic and practiced medicine for fifty years. She always believed that motherhood was her greatest blessing and duty, so she kept her children with her and taught them to be her assistants. Throughout her work, Ellis delivered more than 5,000 babies. She also opened a school of nursing and obstetrics and trained more than 500 nurses. In addition, Ellis traveled throughout the US, Canada, and Mexico, teaching and practicing medicine.

In all she did, Ellis put the Lord first and always prayed for His guidance and blessings. She worked hard to serve all her life.

GREEN FLAKE

1828-1903

"In my Father's house are many mansions." (John 14:2)

Green was born a slave on a plantation in North Carolina. When he was a young man, both he and his master, James Madison Flake, heard the gospel and chose to be baptized. After being baptized, Green went with James to join the Saints in Nauvoo.

When the Saints were moving to the West, Green was chosen as one of a select few to be part of the vanguard party, the first wagons to travel to Utah. Green was known for being strong, trustworthy, and hardworking. He helped construct roads and bridges along the way to make a path for future pioneers. He also drove Brigham Young's wagon and was in the first wagon to enter the Salt Lake Valley. In Utah, Green eventually became a free man, had a family, and owned a farm. He was often honored and remembered as one of the first pioneers to reach Utah and was a popular speaker at Pioneer Day celebrations.

Despite trials from living as a slave for much of his life in a time of widespread racism, Green remained an active member of his ward and a faithful Saint to the end of his days. When he passed away, many important Utah newspapers published the event. Green was buried with his wife beneath a gravestone he carved himself bearing the scripture verse "In my Father's house are many mansions," a final testament to Green's faith in eternal life.

MERE METE WHAANGA

1848-1944

*"Have patience for all things
lie in the hand of God."*

Mere grew up as a member of an important Maori tribe in New Zealand and went on to marry a chief. Although she had power and a high position, her heart was soft and humble.

When the missionaries came to New Zealand, their teachings touched Mere's heart. She convinced her husband, Hirini, to listen to them, and soon they were both baptized. Within a few weeks, hundreds of members of their tribe were baptized as well. Mere and Hirini put their whole hearts into building up the gospel in their homeland. They built a home beside theirs to house missionaries, and Mere cooked and did laundry for them. One missionary referred to Mere as his Maori mother. Often, missionaries would come to Mere for help understanding the Maori language and culture. Mere and Hirini helped the missionaries for many years. Then they received a blessing that they would join the Saints in Utah and work in the temple. Although they would leave behind their large extended family and homeland, Mere and her family pressed forward with faith. They sacrificed and prepared and eventually moved to Utah, becoming the first Maori Saints there. They donated their home in New Zealand to become a permanent home for missionaries.

Mere missed her extended family terribly, and she had some struggles adjusting to life in a new land with a different culture. But eventually she and her husband and children were settled in Salt Lake City. She and Hirini were sealed in the temple and then focused their time on doing temple work for deceased Maori people. Later, Hirini served a mission to New Zealand. After his death, Mere served as a missionary in New Zealand too, and she was known for her strong faith and the way she helped unify and encourage people.

KARL G. MAESER

1828-1901

"This life is one great object lesson to practice on the principles of immortality and eternal life."

Karl grew up in Germany, which had some of the most advanced schools in Europe at the time. He attended an inspiring teachers' college that prepared him well for his future service.

At the time, missionaries were forbidden to enter Germany, and any who tried were arrested. A true miracle led Karl to the restored gospel: He came upon a booklet condemning the Latter-day Saints. However, Karl's soul was touched by what he read. He wanted to learn more about the gospel and soon desired to be baptized. Karl began writing letters requesting missionaries to come teach him. Although it was dangerous, one missionary was sent. Soon, Karl and a handful of others were baptized, and a branch was organized with Karl as the leader.

Eventually, Karl and his family joined the Saints in Utah. There, Karl became known as a gifted teacher. Brigham Young asked him to start a Church school in Provo, Utah—Brigham Young Academy, which would one day become Brigham Young University. President Young said, "Brother Maeser, I want you to remember that you ought not to teach even the alphabet or the multiplication tables without the Spirit of God." Karl took these words to heart and built up a school that aimed to educate both the minds and spirits of every student, inspiring each to become a noble servant of God. Karl inspired countless students with his knowledge, passion for learning, strong moral character, and loving heart. His students would go on to become General Authorities, federal and state politicians, university presidents, and inspiring teachers.

Karl believed his call to teach was sacred, and he fulfilled it with honor. He established hundreds of religious classes, began the Church Educational System, and founded dozens of schools, several of which still operate as universities today.

ELIZABETH CLARIDGE McCUNE

1852-1924

"While abroad I always had a burning desire in my heart to give our Father's children what I knew to be the Truth."

Elizabeth was just a baby when her family left England to join the Saints in Utah. When she was a teenager, her father was called to the "Muddy" mission to settle a desolate part of southern Nevada. She cried when she heard the news because she would miss her home and friends, but she was determined to help her father answer the call with faith. In Nevada, she worked hard and carried every brick and pail of mortar needed to build their new home. Elizabeth said, "I was proud of the fact that I was able to lighten [my father's] burden in some measure."

When Elizabeth was in her forties, she planned to visit family in England and gather genealogical records. She asked President Lorenzo Snow for a blessing before she left and was told, "Thy mind shall be as clear as an angel's when explaining the principles of the Gospel." During her months in England, Elizabeth went out with the missionaries and sang at their street meetings. She felt a strong desire to preach and share the gospel. At a large Church conference in London, her chance came. Antichurch teachings and literature had been harming the spread of the gospel, especially with rumors that women in Utah were badly treated. During the conference, Elizabeth was called upon to share her experiences as a Utah woman. Although she was frightened, she prayed and was able to bear testimony and teach clearly. Word of her influence reached Church leaders in Salt Lake City. At the same time, mission leaders were requesting sister missionaries to help in the mission field. Shortly after, the first full-time proselyting sister missionaries were called.

After returning home, Elizabeth continued to share her testimony and serve. She worked for twenty years in the temple and helped greatly promote and improve family history work throughout the Church.

MELITÓN GONZÁLEZ TREJO

1843–1917

"Go ye into all the world, and preach the gospel to every creature." (Mark 16:15)

Melitón was born in Spain. The son of a city mayor, he attended military school and became an officer in the Spanish Army. While serving, he heard about a group of people following a modern-day prophet in the United States. His heart was touched, and he longed to join them.

Melitón took a position in the Philippines to get him closer to the Saints. For a time, he became distracted by his new work. But then he came down with a sickness. He prayed to the Lord, asking what he should do. In response, Melitón received a special dream from God. Although he felt strong ties to his country and his work, he knew what he needed to do. It was time to join the Saints in America. Melitón left all he knew and traveled to Utah. Two weeks later, he was baptized. At the time, President Brigham Young was preparing to send missionaries to Mexico, and they were in desperate need of help from a native Spanish speaker. Melitón filled this need and began helping to translate the Book of Mormon and other Church materials into Spanish. Later, Melitón joined the early missionaries sent to Mexico. Traveling to Mexico was dangerous, but Melitón had faith in his call. Soon, he and his companion found and baptized the first Mexican converts.

Melitón continued to share the gospel and serve the Lord all his life. He helped settle one of the Church colonies in Mexico and then went to Arizona. Because of his work, millions are able to learn the gospel in their native tongue.

TSUNE ISHIDA NACHIE

1856–1938

"[Many] have felt the force of her great spirit and the tenderness of her love." (Castle H. Murphy, mission president in Hawaii)

Tsune was born in Japan and widowed at a young age. At the time, missionaries were new to Japan, and they were looking for a mission-home housekeeper and cook. Amazingly, Tsune took the job even though she had twenty years of experience in more sophisticated work and could have made more money elsewhere. What the elders didn't know was that Tsune was secretly investigating the Church. She had been attending Sunday School and was touched by what she heard. As she worked in the mission home, she quietly learned about the gospel. After just a month of work, she told the missionaries she wanted to be baptized. They thought she needed more time to learn, but Tsune was determined. She had found new light and meaning through the gospel and wasn't going to let it go. She was soon baptized in a stream and was filled with joy.

Tsune loved her new faith and wanted to share it with everyone. One by one, she invited friends to stay with her at the mission home, where she taught them the gospel. Several of her friends and family members felt the Spirit and were baptized.

When Tsune was old, many of the missionaries she had cared for pooled money together so that she could fulfill her dream of attending the temple in Hawaii. She did so and retired in Hawaii so that she could focus on temple work. Tsune was the first Japanese convert to enter the temple and the first Japanese temple worker. But she didn't stop there. She also served as an active member missionary, going out daily with a basket of Church materials to teach Japanese immigrants in Hawaii. Because of her, the gospel grew among Japanese Hawaiians. Tsune left a lasting legacy of faith and love.

JAMES E. TALMAGE

1862–1933

"Within the gospel of Jesus Christ, there is room and place for all truth thus far learned by man or yet to be made known."

James was born in England and raised in the gospel. However, his baptism was delayed for various reasons, and at age ten he still had not been baptized. During that year, James became dangerously sick. His father prayed and covenanted with God that if James were healed, he would be baptized right away. James recovered, and his baptism was planned. It was the first step on a lifelong path of following Jesus Christ.

Still, James's baptism did not happen easily. Because of persecution against the Saints, his family planned the baptism at night. When they snuck to the water's edge, they heard a terrible, horrifying shriek and howl in the darkness. James's father asked if he was too afraid to be baptized. James recalled, "I answered by stepping into the water." Immediately the screaming sound stopped, and James became a member of Christ's restored Church.

A few years later, James and his family traveled to America to join the Saints in Utah. There, James attended Brigham Young Academy. An excellent student, he was able to graduate with nearly perfect scores and become a teacher by age sixteen. James was a noted scholar and often used his skills to build up God's kingdom. For example, the First Presidency asked him to write a detailed book about Jesus Christ. James worked diligently in a special room in the temple, writing by hand on the backs of old legal documents because there was a paper shortage. In the end, *Jesus the Christ* became a seven-hundred-page masterpiece all about the Savior's life and ministry.

Throughout his life, James earned many honors and positions, yet he chose to put the Lord first. He served as an Apostle for over twenty years, and his books and teachings are still loved and used to this day, helping teach and spread the gospel.

MARTHA "MATTIE" HUGHES CANNON

1857-1932

"I know that this is His work and that what we are passing through is for our benefit."

Mattie was born in Wales and traveled with her family to Zion when she was just one year old. She was passionate and motivated and chose to pursue higher education at a time when doing so was uncommon for women. She attended medical school and also received degrees in pharmacy and elocution. She was the only female student in the pharmacy program. Soon she began work as a doctor and was the resident physician at Deseret Hospital.

Mattie loved to help others and was concerned about public health. She decided to run for the Utah State Senate and won, beating her own husband for the seat and becoming the first female state senator in the United States. She served for two terms, using her position to help others. She focused on making laws to protect vulnerable groups. Many of her efforts still affect Utah today and were revolutionary in the field of public health. She put forward the bills to create the first Utah Department of Health and a state school for the deaf, mute, and blind. She also promoted bills to improve working conditions for women and campaigned for women's rights throughout her life.

Mattie spent many years living in exile because she chose to accept the call to practice polygamy, but she never lost her passion for helping others. She spent her final years volunteering her medical skills to help people struggling with addictions. To this day she is honored and remembered for her many great works.

HENRY EYRING

1901–1981

"Contemplating this awe-inspiring order extending from the almost infinitely small to the infinitely large, one is overwhelmed with its grandeur and with the limitless wisdom which conceived, created and governs it all."

Henry grew up as a cattle rancher and farmer in Mexico and Arizona, where his parents raised him to work hard and have great faith. His mother often told him, "Henry, I hope you'll not just be good but that you'll be good for something." Although Henry would eventually be known as one of the great scientists of the twentieth century, he never forgot his early life lessons and worked hard to do good and serve the Lord.

Henry received many honors and awards as a scientist, yet he made time to focus on spiritual teaching and learning, too. While working at Princeton University, he took time to preach the gospel in the university common area to anyone willing to listen. Henry also helped Saints struggling to understand how science and religion fit together. As Henry said, "For me, there has been no serious difficulty in reconciling the principles of true science with the principles of true religion." Henry wrote a book titled *The Faith of a Scientist* to show how religion and faith are connected. One German Saint wrote to Henry about how the book had helped his father, a mathematician. The boy's father loved Henry's book and chose to be baptized a year after reading it.

Throughout his life, Henry worked as a professor in prestigious universities, wrote more than 600 articles and textbooks, and worked with prominent scientists around the world. One of his theories, the Absolute Rate Theory, is known as one of the most important scientific theories of its time and continues to impact numerous scientific fields. Along the way, Henry balanced his career with family life and Church service. Cheerfully and faithfully, he chose to pursue truth in all its forms, inspiring others to do the same.

COHN SHOSHONITZ ZUNDEL

1863–1949

"Jesus is coming. . . . While you are waiting, go do your work and read and learn all you can."

Cohn, a member of the Northwestern Band of the Shoshone Nation, was born in a time of great change for her people. Just months before her birth, her family survived the Bear River Massacre, in which nearly all of her tribe members were killed. After the massacre, only around 150 members of Cohn's band were left. In the midst of their heartache, the tribe learned about the gospel and were baptized. The Church then helped the tribe establish a farming community, Washakie, where Cohn lived throughout her life.

Cohn was one of the earliest Native American Church members. She was present when President Eliza R. Snow and future prophet Lorenzo Snow came to organize the Relief Society in her branch at Washakie. During the visit, Cohn was called as the Relief Society second counselor. She went on to serve as a leader in her branch's Relief Society for more than thirty-five years, teaching and inspiring her fellow members. She was known for her strong testimony and for encouraging others to follow the gospel.

In addition to serving in the Church, Cohn worked hard to serve her family. She lived as a widow for nearly fifty years, and several of her children died young. Still, she was generous and had a good sense of humor. She made special baked sugar beets to share with children. She also loved to do traditional hide tanning, beadwork, and moccasin sewing. Most important, she taught her children and grandchildren to have faith. One of her granddaughters remembered a hard winter when Cohn told her not to worry about food. Cohn said all would be well, and their prayers would be answered. She was right. Cohn stayed true to her faith all her life, working hard and passing on her beliefs to her family and community.

KIM HO JIK

1905–1959

"I know of a gospel—a wonderful gospel—capable of giving you new hope, new life."

From his boyhood in Korea, Ho Jik felt a spiritual hunger. He investigated many churches and even studied in a Buddhist monastery. Eventually, he joined a Protestant church, but he still had unanswered questions. It wasn't until he traveled to the United States to study for his PhD that he found the answers he was seeking.

Ho Jik was studying nutritional science at Cornell University when he noticed that one of his fellow students was different. This classmate, Oliver Wayman, kept the Word of Wisdom, and he worked hard, but never on Sundays. Ho Jik wanted to know why. Soon, with Oliver's help, he gained a testimony of the restored gospel and chose to be baptized, becoming the first Korean member of the Church. At his baptism in 1951, he heard a voice say to him, "Feed my sheep, feed my sheep." Ho Jik returned to Korea knowing he had a special work to do.

Back in Korea, Ho Jik worked hard and became a notable figure, working as a professor, as a university president, and eventually as Korea's vice minister of education. With all his worldly success, he never lost his focus on God. In fact, he used his positions and influence to help the gospel spread. Because of Ho Jik, the Church was officially recognized in Korea and missionaries were allowed into the country much sooner than expected. Ho Jik shared the gospel every chance he got and even preached about the gospel when invited to speak in a nationwide academic Korean broadcast. Ho Jik helped teach with the missionaries, translated Church materials into Korean, and served in many Church callings, including as president of the Korean District of the Northern Far East Mission. He kept his faith burning bright all his life and never forgot his call to feed the Savior's sheep in Korea.

MINERVA TEICHERT

1888-1976

"I promised the Lord if I'd finished my work and he'd give me some more, I'd gladly do it. With this covenant in my heart I began to live."

When Minerva was just four years old, growing up on her family's ranch in Idaho, she received her first set of paints. From then on, she knew she was an artist and carried art supplies with her everywhere. She loved the wild beauty of the West and often rode out on her horse to sketch and paint landscapes. Later, Minerva worked all sorts of odd jobs, from sketching for medical schools to performing rope tricks and dances, to pay for art school. She studied art in both Chicago and New York with famous artists and became a top student. Minerva was poised to make a name for herself as a great artist, but she chose to put faith and family before fame.

Back home, she married, raised a family, and helped run her ranch, but she never stopped painting. She would even add bits to her paintings in the middle of cooking supper. Minerva felt called to tell the story of her faith and the epic pioneer experience through her art.

In her middle years, Minerva received a commission to paint forty-two murals based on Book of Mormon stories. She threw herself into the huge task, working from 1949 to 1951. Of the project, Minerva said, "[It is the] greatest joy as well as the toughest job I ever hope to undertake."

Minerva used her unique talents to bring stories of faith to life. Although she had great skills, she was loving, generous, and humble. She sold many of her paintings to BYU to pay tuition for her children, grandchildren, and other young people, and she gave away paintings as gifts. Her art can be seen in museums, temples, chapels, and Church manuals throughout the world. Minerva's faith lives on through the painting she loved and the hearts her work touches.

1913-2008

"The translation was done through much prayer and fasting . . . also through the Holy Ghost and power from on high."

Wei-I, a humble man from Taiwan, China, who earned just enough money to get by, was prepared by the Lord for a special work. Although he never attended high school or college, he once served as a military colonel and could speak and read both English and Mandarin Chinese. His knowledge and humility were just the things the Lord needed to build up His Church in China.

When missionaries first came to Taiwan, China, in 1956, the work was difficult. There were very few Church materials available in Chinese, and there was still no Chinese translation of the Book of Mormon. One day, two of the elders serving in Taipei prayed to be guided to someone to teach. That prayer led them down a small side street to Wei-I's door. From the very beginning, Wei-I was open and willing to learn. One of the missionaries gave Wei-I several Church books in English, and Wei-I began to study them and share them with others. After a few months, he chose to be baptized.

From then on, Wei-I embarked on a life of service to the Lord. He served in his branch presidency, as a temple sealer, and as the first patriarch in Taiwan, China. Perhaps his greatest service was in translating the first Chinese edition of the Book of Mormon. For years, others had attempted to translate the Book of Mormon into Chinese without success. In 1963, Wei-I was called by Elder Gordon B. Hinckley to take on the work. Wei-I worked diligently, even taking time off from work without pay so he could focus on the translation. After seven months, the work was complete. As a result, hundreds of millions of people could now read the Book of Mormon in their native language.

KASIMIRA VIKTORIA CWIKLINSKI WURSCHER

1897–1991

"In these difficult times, we especially felt the help of our Heavenly Father. Always when our need was greatest, His help was nearest."

Kasimira grew up in Berlin, Germany, and lived through World War I, World War II, and life in Communist East Germany. She experienced many personal tragedies and witnessed the suffering of others. But hard things did not make her bitter. Instead, they taught her to cling to the Lord and show compassion to others.

Some of Kasimira's earliest tragedies were the deaths of her two-year-old son and newborn daughter. After they died, Kasimira took long walks to ease her pain. On one of these walks, she met the missionaries. They taught her that her children were not gone forever—she would see them again. Kasimira believed their words and invited them to teach her family. In 1924, she and her husband, Otto, were baptized. After being baptized, Kasimira poured her heart into serving God. Difficult things kept happening, such as two sons dying in World War II and her youngest child dying of illness. During these times, Kasimira's grief was strong, but her faith was stronger. She said that in her darkest times she felt lifted up by Heavenly Father, and she developed a special compassion for others who were suffering.

After World War II, Kasimira was called as the president of the East German Mission Relief Society. She served in that role for over twenty years, speaking and traveling to strengthen the Saints. She was especially mindful of those who were ill, elderly, and bedridden, and she often visited them in their homes. She developed special relationships with many of these sisters, and one described her as having a "face as bright as sunshine." Kasimira's own heartaches had taught her to have love and concern for others. She continued serving God and His children faithfully all her life.

HELMUTH HÜBENER

1925–1942

*"I know that God lives and
He will be the Just Judge in this matter."*

Helmuth grew up in Hamburg, Germany, the son of a single mother who worked hard to get by. He loved to study world history, politics, and geography, and he excelled in school. He was also a devoted member of the Church.

When Helmuth was a young teenager, the Nazi government took over Germany. Helmuth didn't agree with the hateful, oppressive ways of the Nazis. When war broke out in 1939, Helmuth told his close friend Rudi, "The fire has started to burn—in Poland now—but soon the whole world will be in flames." Helmuth began an apprenticeship with the civil service, where he had access to forbidden books that helped him learn more about the outside world. Then, when he was sixteen, everything changed. Helmuth's older brother gave him a powerful radio, and he was able to listen to forbidden news broadcasts from outside Germany. He discovered many lies the Nazis were telling the German people, and knew he needed to share the truth. Helmuth recruited his two closest friends from Church, and together they began sharing what they heard on the radio. Helmuth took notes and created pamphlets that he and his friends secretly placed in mailboxes, on bulletin boards, and even into people's pockets. Spreading these pamphlets was dangerous, but Helmuth and his friends believed they were choosing the right. Helmuth wrote more than sixty pamphlets exposing the lies of the Nazi government.

After several months, the secret police figured out who was behind the pamphlets. Helmuth and his friends were arrested. During the trial, Helmuth seemed to draw attention to himself to save his friends. They received lighter sentences, but Helmuth was condemned to death. Courageous to the end, he died trusting that he had done the right thing and would soon be with his Heavenly Father.

MARJORIE PAY HINCKLEY

1911-2004

"If I can just be one more voice to say that God lives and that this is His work, I will be satisfied."

Marjorie grew up in a home full of faith. She went to church on Sundays, prayed, and listened to stories of her pioneer ancestors. Hanging in her bedroom was a picture of the boy Jesus in the temple. It was the first thing she saw when she woke each morning, and she looked at the picture as her mother read her stories about Jesus. Little by little, Marjorie's love for the Savior grew.

When Marjorie was seventeen, she received her first real Church calling as a children's Sunday School teacher. At first, she was excited and got to work right away on her lesson. But then she started to worry. How could she teach children about things she didn't yet know for sure? Marjorie talked to her father, and he advised her to read Joseph Smith's First Vision account and see how she felt. Up in her room, Marjorie reread the story of young Joseph Smith. She knew it well, but this time she was reading with a heart yearning to know the truth. As she finished reading about Heavenly Father and Jesus coming to Joseph, she felt peaceful inside. She knew that what Joseph said he had experienced truly did happen, and she was ready to teach it to others.

Throughout her life, Marjorie continued to bear her testimony, eventually speaking to people all over the world when she traveled with her husband, President Gordon B. Hinckley, the fifteenth President of the Church. Countless people remember her for her strong and steady faith, the way she bore her testimony, and her optimistic attitude. She was known for saying, "Things always work out somehow." Side by side with her husband, she did all she could to build up the Lord's kingdom and share her bright faith.

ANTHONY OBINNA

1928-1995

"God is great and performs wonders. No human power can withhold God's work in this world."

Anthony grew up in a Nigerian village. He was one of the few children in his area to receive a formal education. Eventually, he began to work as a schoolteacher, but he would soon teach more than math and reading.

Beginning in 1965, Anthony had three special dreams. In the dreams, he was visited by a person who showed him a beautiful building. Later, Anthony saw the building in a magazine—it was the Salt Lake Temple! Anthony yearned to know more, but Nigeria was in the midst of a civil war. He had to wait six years for the war to end before he could write a letter to the Church in Salt Lake City. The Church sent him pamphlets and a Book of Mormon but said missionaries could not come to Nigeria at that time. Anthony was disappointed and also suffered persecution for his new beliefs. But he chose to hold to his new faith. He said, "I knew I had discovered the truth, and men's threats could not move me." Anthony began to share the gospel with others. Many of his family and friends gained testimonies of their own. They waited with hope, prayer, and faith.

Finally, years later, missionaries arrived in Nigeria. Anthony was overjoyed. At that time, he had helped more than seventy people learn about the restored gospel, and many were ready for baptism. When Anthony and his wife were baptized, they became the first black members of the Church in West Africa.

Because of faithful Saints like Anthony, many, many people were prepared to receive the gospel when missionaries began coming to African countries. Anthony rejoiced in all he had received from God and served with love the rest of his days.

JULIA MAVIMBELA

1917–2000

"Let us dig the soil of bitterness, throw in a seed of love, and see what fruits it can give us. . . . Love will not come without forgiving others."

Julia grew up in South Africa during times of great inequality and conflict. Despite poverty and other challenges, she worked hard to gain an education, becoming a teacher and eventually one of the first black female school principals in South Africa. She fell in love with a wonderful man and had many children. Life was going well, but soon Julia would face great challenges.

When Julia had several children at home and another on the way, her husband, John, was killed in a tragic car accident for which he was blamed, even though he was clearly not at fault. For years, Julia struggled with pain and bitterness from this experience. But she refused to let bitterness rule her heart. Instead, she said, "I found a way of getting myself away from the worries of these years, and that was through community involvement."

One of Julia's greatest community projects was working with youth. At the time, there was great racial conflict in South Africa, and many youth were full of fear and anger. Julia began community gardens as a way of helping the youth heal. She taught important gardening skills while also teaching the youth to let go of hatred and learn to forgive. She taught them how, just like the hard earth, hard hearts can be softened so that beautiful things can grow.

Throughout Julia's life, she gave service. She established many organizations to help women, yet she still missed her husband and felt pain deep inside. Then at last she found healing in an unexpected place: she met two missionaries during a community clean-up project. The missionaries taught her about ordinances for the dead and God's plan for eternal families. Finally, Julia felt full peace and joy. She embraced the gospel, and ever after, she continued her life of service.

HELVÉCIO MARTINS

1930-2005

*"We had found the truth,
and nothing would stop us from living it."*

When Helvécio was a young boy in Brazil, his family fell on hard times. At twelve years old, he chose to leave school and start working to help his family. Although those early years were difficult, Helvécio later said that learning to work hard was a great blessing in his life.

Helvécio eventually married a woman named Ruda, and they started a family together. They both wanted to come closer to God, and they prayed and prayed for guidance. One night, Helvécio was stuck in a traffic jam. He got out of his car, looked up to the sky, and prayed for help in finding the truth and joy he and his family were seeking. God heard his cry, and two weeks later the missionaries showed up at Helvécio's door. Their first visit lasted over four hours. By the end, Helvécio felt peace and knew he had found the answers he was seeking. He and his family were soon baptized.

From then on, Helvécio worked hard to serve God, even when it was difficult. Within two weeks he began serving as a Sunday School teacher. A few years later, he was called to serve on the publicity committee for the São Paulo Temple, even though, at the time, members with black African ancestry like Helvécio were still not permitted to enter the temple or hold the priesthood. Helvécio chose to trust the Lord and press on in faith. He and his wife felt the Spirit on the temple grounds, and Ruda even sold her jewelry to help raise funds for the temple. They never expected to enter the temple in their lifetime, but then revelation came in 1978 making the priesthood available to all worthy male members and allowing all worthy members to receive all the ordinances of the temple. Helvécio and his family were sealed in the temple, and their son went on to serve a mission. Years later, Helvécio was called as a member of the Seventy, making him the first modern General Authority with black African ancestry.

MORE STANDOUT SAINTS

JOHN TAYLOR (1808–1887), third President of the Church, went with Joseph and Hyrum Smith to Carthage Jail, helped build up the Church in Canada and Europe

MARIA JACKSON NORMINGTON (1820–1881), faithful, determined pioneer in Martin handcart company, crawled on elbows and knees when her feet were too frozen for walking, rescued a man left for dead on the trail

TRUMAN O. ANGELL (1810–1887), architect, dedicated his talents to God, worked on the Kirtland and Nauvoo Temples, served as Church architect for the Salt Lake and St. George Temples as well as many other noted buildings

CORA GEORGIANA SNOW (1843–1887), one of the first female lawyers in Utah, later served on Utah Supreme Court, traveled across the plains as a young girl

JAMES C. FLETCHER (1919–1991), noted scientist and faithful Saint, served as head of NASA and University of Utah president

MAUD MAY BABCOCK (1867–1954), "First Lady of Utah Theater," first female professor at University of Utah, produced more than three hundred plays, organized first college dramatic club, gave dedicated service to Church and to the deaf and blind

STEPHEN R. COVEY (1932–2012), inspirational leader and teacher, wrote the best-selling book *The Seven Habits of Highly Effective People,* which sold more than 25 million copies

AMANDA INEZ KNIGHT (1876–1937) and LUCY JANE BRIMHALL (1875–1957), the first single, full-time proselytizing sister missionaries, served faithfully in England, later became community and Church leaders

JOSEPH W. B. JOHNSON (1934–2012), early gospel pioneer in Ghana, gained a testimony and received a vision, spread the gospel and built up congregations in Ghana many years before missionaries arrived

ANICETA FAJARDO (1890–?), first member of the Church in the Philippines, baptized before missionaries were officially sent to the Philippines

JAMES C. CHRISTENSEN (1942–2017), famous painter, known for his detailed work and rich religious symbolism

SRILAKSANA SUNTARAHUT (1924–2013), early convert in Thailand, primary translator of the Book of Mormon, Doctrine and Covenants, and Pearl of Great Price into Thai, an eager missionary who helped build up the Church

KREŠIMIR ĆOSIĆ (1948–1995), legendary basketball player from Yugoslavia, translated the Book of Mormon and Doctrine and Covenants into Croatian, worked as a peace activist and diplomat

LILLIAN ASHBY (1938–1976), faithful missionary who shared the gospel while dying of cancer, instrumental in bringing the gospel to India

RESOURCES TO EXPLORE

- Church History Museum, located in Salt Lake City, Utah https://history.churchofjesuschrist.org/section/museum
- Church History website https://history.churchofjesuschrist.org/
- Doctrine and Covenants story videos https://www.churchofjesuschrist.org/children/videos/scripture-stories/doctrine-and-covenants
- *Exploring the Pioneer Trail: A Flashlight Discovery Book*, by Shauna Gibby
- FamilySearch (free family history tools) https://www.familysearch.org/
- Global Histories (Church history stories from around the world) https://history.churchofjesuschrist.org/landing/global-histories
- Inspiring movies from Church history, including *17 Miracles*, *Ephraim's Rescue*, and *The Other Side of Heaven*
- *My First Church History Stories*, by Deanna Draper Buck
- Pearl of Great Price Coloring Book (free PDF) https://www.churchofjesuschrist.org/children/scripture-stories/coloring-book/pearl-of-great-price
- Pioneers in Every Land (inspiring short films and stories about faithful Saints around the world) https://history.churchofjesuschrist.org/section/pioneers
- Prophet Videos (minifilms about prophets of the latter days) https://www.churchofjesuschrist.org/children/videos-music/prophet
- Sing-along Church music videos, including *To Be a Pioneer* https://www.churchofjesuschrist.org/children/music/music-videos?lang=eng&videoId=6044180927001

SELECTED BIBLIOGRAPHY

- *BYU Studies Quarterly*, multiple journal volumes
- Church History resources https://history.churchofjesuschrist.org/
- *Daughters in My Kingdom: The History and Work of Relief Society*
- *Elect Ladies: Presidents of the Relief Society*, by LaRene Gaunt and Janet Peterson
- *Ensign, Liahona, New Era,* and *Friend* magazines
- *Heroes of the Restoration*, compilation
- *History of the Saints: Signs, Wonders, and Miracles: Extraordinary Stories from Early Latter-day Saints*, edited by Glenn Rawson and Dennis Lyman
- *Saints, Volume 1: The Standard of Truth, 1815–1846*
- *We'll Bring the World His Truth: Missionary Adventures from Around the World*, by Dean Hughes and Tom Hughes
- *Women of Character: Profiles of 100 Prominent LDS Women*, by Mary Jane Woodger and Susan Easton Black
- *Women of Faith in the Latter Days,* volumes 1–4, edited by Richard E. Turley Jr. and Brittany Chapman Nash

ACKNOWLEDGMENTS

There are so many people I want to thank! First, I have to thank my wonderful husband, Chris, who supported me all through this long project and was my first sounding board. I also want to thank my critique partners and many other friends and family members who read and commented on early drafts of this work and shared their enthusiasm for it. Special thanks go to the amazing professors in BYU's Department of Asian and Near Eastern Languages who helped me track down and translate crucial information about Hu Wei-I. In addition, I want to thank Virginia Pearce Cowley for her help with Marjorie Pay Hinckley's biography. Thanks are also due to all of the historians and researchers whose work I studied.

I also want to thank the wonderful team at Deseret Book, especially Celia Barnes, who worked with me through several early drafts and championed the project, as well as my editor, Emily Watts. Finally, I want to thank all the pioneers and Standout Saints—those I was privileged to learn and write about and those whose stories are still to be told. Their faith, strength, and courage are an endless well of inspiration. Last but not least, thank you to my Heavenly Father and Savior for all the blessings we've received in these last days, for the beautiful gospel, and for the guidance, strength, and love They give me.

ABOUT THE AUTHOR

SIERRA WILSON is the daughter of two amazing modern-day pioneers who embraced the restored gospel as teenagers and never looked back. She loves studying history and used to teach ancient world history to ninth graders. Now she works part-time as an author/illustrator and full-time as a mom of four wild and wonderful little ones. Sierra wrote the picture book *The Atonement of Jesus Christ Is for Me* and has two new gospel-themed picture books coming out soon. You can learn more about her and her work at www.sierrawilsonauthor.com or connect with her on social media.

ABOUT THE ILLUSTRATOR

EMILY SHAY TUELLER is a freelance illustrator based in Cedar Hills, Utah. After receiving awards throughout her education for her art, she decided to make a passionate career of it. Since then her artwork has found its way into thousands of homes throughout the world. Emily has a unique approach in blending digital, whimsical, and fine art. She is mom to three kids under the age of five, home being quite the ruckus. Emily also enjoys spending time in the mountains and being silly with her family. You can find more information about Emily at @emilyshayart and www.emilyshayart.etsy.com.